The Cockatoo Dictionary A Few Words More

Tom Klingenfuss

IVEUGWQMCSIOK.XLIKW
FOYZLXUSPEJNJXUIOUBT
QDAYCUMUDWSJDQLBW
SGHOFHRYX.

Achnivers-

Plural Noun

[ahk-nih-vers]

men who think that watching sports is relatively boring

Afmiralding-

Verb

[af-mer-ahl-deeng]

when a person says yes but actually means no

Alfortize-

Verb

[al-fer-ties]

when a man puts his principals before his benefit or wellbeing

Anderpal-

Noun

[an-der-pull]
an idiotic person who will attend social gatherings even when they are sick

Arashol-

Noun

[are-uh-shawl]

a male fictional character that portrays true masculinity

Arnudus-

Noun

[are-noo-duhs]

a guy that betrays one of his friends when it comes to the pursuit of a girl

Azulots-

Plural Noun

[ah-zoo-luhts]

people who have political ideologies as their religion

Banchardize-

Verb

[bahn-cher-dies]
the action of race swapping a character in an adaption of a work of fiction

Charconnel-

Noun

[char-cah-nehl]

a smoker whose clothes, car, living space and all other possessions smell like smoke

Ciractums-

Plural Noun

[ser-ahk-tuhms]

politically incorrect terms that are now politically correct

Cliaganons-

Plural Noun

[klee-ah-guh-nawns]

people who manage to get prescribed medication for mental illnesses that they don't have

Codisterate-

Verb

[koe-dih-ster-aet]

the act of helping someone achieve cognitive dissonance

Cosocizals-

Plural Noun

[koe-suh-kie-zuhls]
men that have
never asked a
girl out in person

Dantasbol-

Noun

[dahn-taz-bole]

an exceptionally good day

Delbusfal-

Verb

[dehl-boos-full]

the action of a company blaming their customers for not liking a product

Difigasure-

Verb

[dih-fih-guh-sher]

when a person insists on you giving them a different reason than the actual reason you already gave them

Dirmup-

Noun

[der-mup]

a coffee mug that is stained beyond the point of cleaning

Dismentous-

Noun

[dis-men-shoo-us]

a person who blatantly lies in an attempt to win an argument

Dogalip-

Noun

[daw-guh-lip]
a man that makes promises to a woman which he has no intentions of keeping

Edimortian-

Noun

[eh-dih-more-shun]

a person who will eat themself to the point of death

Ediprefan-

Noun

[eh-dih-preh-fihn]

a person who propagates the idea that a morbidly obese person is a healthy individual

Enfosals-

Plural Noun

[en-foe-sahls]
obese individuals who think that buildings and modes of transportation should be redesigned for their three person plus sized self

Exfamur-

Noun

[ehks-fah-mer]

a woman that uses her pregnancy as an excuse to eat for five

Falwistment-

Noun

[fal-whist-mehnt]

when the Pope says or does things that don't line up with God's character in the bible

Famerupt-

Noun

[fah-mer-upt]
promotions and hirings based on identity politics as opposed to merit

Fesponse-

Noun

[feh-spawnse]

a response from a female that falls within the female response window

Finswers–

Plural Noun

[fihn-swers]

people who will gladly pay money to be lied to

Fowliperans-

Plural Noun

[fow-lih-per-ihns]
fashion choices
or societal
trends that
women partake
in which men
don't understand

Friediplines-

Plural Noun

[free-dih-plihns]

people on diets that never follow the diets

Fulipticants-

Plural Noun

[fool-ihp-tih-kahnts]

girl bosses who are under the misconception that they are completely independent from men

Gawnatic-

Noun

[gaw-nah-tick]
a terrible sense
of style, or
perhaps the lack
thereof

Gludelical-

Noun

[gloo-dehl-ih-kuhl]
food for healthy
diets that
actually tastes
good

Gobmorit-

Noun

[gawb-more-iht]

a gobsurded individual that has no idea that they're an annoying simpleton

Golmacers-

Plural Noun

[gole-mae-sers] minorities in western civilization who think that all "white people" are the same despite their different ethnicities

Grimastery-

Noun

[grih-mah-ster-ee]
the stereotype that Germans are very good at telling stories

Gwidoral-

Noun

[gwih-der-ahl]

a man that is suicidal because he lacks purpose of any sort

Hafeligates-

Plural Noun

[hah-feh-lih-gehts] modern day criminals who lack professionalism

Hypluttons-

Plural Noun

[hih-pluh-tehns]

Christians who fail to recognize that gluttony is a sin

Invacnagent-

Noun

[ihn-vahk-nuh-jehnt]

acne wash that creates an acne problem as opposed to stopping an acne problem

Jacordisol-

Noun

[jah-core-dih-zole]
an individual that is disrespectful to a server at a restaurant for no reason

Jarafols-

Plural Noun

[jair-uh-fawls]

people who get mad if you don't take their advice, even if it's stupid advice

Jasicknal-

Noun

[jah-sihk-null]

a man that isn't nearly as clever as he thinks he is

Jonethization-

Noun

[joe-nih-thih-zae-shuhn]

a conspiracy theory that turns out to be factually true

Kleaptule-

Noun

[klehp-tool]

the cheapest of cheapskates

Lanantiver-

Noun

[lah-nahn-tih-ver]

an individual that hates swimming

Lemotan-

Noun

[leh-moe-tihn]

television shows with series finales that completely suck

Letimoloquy-

Noun

[leh-tih-mawl-ah-kwee]

a beautifully crafted monologue with a quality that inspires writers to write

Lexperitics-

Plural Noun

[leks-per-ih-tihks] critics and professors who have never done anything worthy of teaching let alone created anything to be criticized by others

Lisectal-

Noun

[lih-sehk-tuhl]

a copout that Christians use for unchristian like conduct

Louwardens-

Plural Noun

[luh-wore-dihns]

men that should be ashamed of themselves for their lack of accountability

Lovexous-

Adjective

[luh-vehk-shoo-us]
when words
can't describe
how beautiful a
girl is, lovexous
is the word use

Mabolist-

Noun

[mah-boe-lihst]

a woman that is as statistically rare as a winning lottery ticket

Madather-

Noun

[muh-dah-ther]

one of the best wingmen a guy could have

Marbenuls-

Plural Noun

[mar-bih-nulls]
movies or shows
that are so
terrible that one
wonders why
they were even
produced in the
first place

Mascuther-

Noun

[mah-skoo-ther]

a man that conducts business with straightforward honesty as opposed to a backwards lack of transparency

Medamorize-

Verb

[meh-dah-mer-ize]
the action of shaming men for being attracted to women that they are biologically hardwired to be attracted to

Mensparensty-

Noun

[mihn-spair-ehn-stee]

the blunt honesty that occurs when there are only men in the room

Milatrophine-

Noun

[mihl-ah-troe-feen]

a person that hates participation trophies

Misnampter-

Noun

[mihs-nahm-ter]

a person that feels uncomfortable with the fact that they have a German last name

Nulabers-

Plural Noun

[null-ah-bers]

arbitrary rules in society followed by people that would benefit from the rules at the expense of others for whom the rules don't apply

Oregaldens-

Plural Noun

[ore-gal-dihns]

corrupt politicians who take money from foreign nations and don't properly cover their tracks out of arrogance

Orthevans-

Plural Noun
[ore-theh-vihns]
acts of hostility from Christian churches towards men in their congregation as well as men in general

Pabomeruces-

Plural Noun

[pah-baw-mer-oos-ehs]

bosses and supervisors who are insecure because of their subordinates' hard work

Podimens-

Plural Noun

[pah-dih-mihns]

terms that are unnecessarily redundant

Porectoralists-

Plural Noun

[pore-ick-tore-uhl-ists]

people who don't believe in world saving causes created by the establishment in order to obtain assets

Predactineer-

Noun

[preh-dack-tih-near]

a person that prepares for every eventuality humanly imaginable

Proparigists-

Plural Noun

[praw-per-ih-jihsts] people who insist that society uses their made-up pronouns

Puldarits-

Plural Noun

[puhl-dair-ihts]

books that are wrongfully mischaracterized by people who have never read them

Qalidonize-

Verb

[kuh-lih-duh-nize]
the action of gender swapping a character in an adaptation of a work of fiction

Randavicks-

Plural Noun

[rahn-deh-vix] people who are completely comfortable with their living space being disgustingly dirty

Randipar-

Noun

[rahn-dih-par]

food that both smells and tastes awful

Remefols-

Plural Noun

[reh-meh-fawls]

lesbians that men wish weren't lesbians

Ressentables-

Plural Noun

[reh-sehn-tuh-bulls]
food that a
person eats for
nourishment as
opposed to
enjoyment

Rixplesmer-

Noun

[rihks-plehs-mer]

a person that actually enjoys exercising

Senbilovine-

Noun

[sin-bill-oh-veen]

a person that can dish it out but can't take it

Shemasticians-

Plural Noun

[sheh-mah-stih-shins]

normal female characters in action movies that don't obey the laws of physics during fight scenes, especially fight scenes against men

Shevoral-

Noun

[sheh-ver-uhl]

a bookcase exclusively filled with books which the owner has never read

Shorismer-

Noun

[shuh-riz-mer]

a person that cannot formulate a valid argument

Snazor-

Noun

[snah-zore]

a person that is very uninteresting to talk to

Spesfortists-

Plural Noun

[speh-fer-tists]

women who have found out that radical feminism is filled with hallow promises

Stractemer-

Noun

[strack-teh-mer]

a schemer without the nefarious connotation or denotation

Systalbens-

Plural Noun

[sih-stull-bihns]

rules that should bend when there is nuance to a given situation

Talactener-

Noun

[tah-lack-tehn-er]

a man of irony

Taudispec-

Noun

[taw-dih-speck]

a man that talks about what he will achieve but never gets around to working on achieving it

Tisorup-

Noun

[tih-sore-up]

toilet paper that has difficulty getting the job done

Tokerest-

Noun

[toe-ker-est]

an individual that lacks the ability to read a room

Tragarons-

Plural Noun

[trah-ger-ons]

women who tell men what type of woman they should be attracted to

Trompavire-

Noun

[trome-puh-veer]

the genre of vampire romance novels

Twocksby-

Noun

[twahx-bee]
the
oversimplification
of a book being
racist, sexist, or
any other "ist" or
"ism" that society
plays fast and
loose with

Valemers-

Plural Noun

[vahl-leh-mers]

streaming platforms that almost no one has heard of

Vandeluf-

Noun

[vahn-dehl-uhf]

a guy that thinks that he's a ladies' man when he truly isn't

Varudners-

Plural Noun

[var-ruhd-ners]

men who age unbelievably well as the decades go by

Waldyrons-

Plural Noun

[wahl-die-ruhns]

internet personalities who don't practice what they preach

Widapols-

Plural Noun

[wih-duh-pulls]

people who think they're special based solely on the genetic traits they were born with

Woluther-

Noun

[wah-loo-ther]
brand new clothing that intentionally looks worn out

Woosanger-

Noun

[wuh-sen-jur]

an individual that expects far more from others than they expect from themselves

Xegolirits-

Plural Noun

[zeh-gawl-er-ihts]

men who are invisible to the majority of women

Yasterlope-

Noun

[yah-stir-lope]

the sitcom trope of the husband being a buffoon while the wife is a genius

Yastesin-

Noun

[yah-steh-sihn] cold cereal that mainly consists of sugar or high fructose corn syrup, and has little to no nutritional value

Zielardy-

Noun

[zih-lar-dee]

a woman that is somehow more unbearable than a sandberschumer

Check out CockatooNews.com, *The Cockatoo Dictionary A Poor Choice of Words, Don't Shoot Me I'm Only The Joke Writer* and the Cockatoo Digitals YouTube Channel.